T0065434

Planting Seeds:

The Art of Witnessing

George W. Baum

WESTBOW
P R E S S®
A DIVISION OF THOMAS NELSON
& ZONDERVAN

WestBow Press books may be ordered through booksellers or by contacting:

WestBow Press
A Division of Thomas Nelson & Zondervan
1663 Liberty Drive
Bloomington, IN 47403
www.westbowpress.com
844-714-3454

Scripture quotations marked NIV are taken from The Holy Bible, New
International Version®, NIV® Copyright © 1973, 1978, 1984, 2011 by
Biblica, Inc.® Used by permission. All rights reserved worldwide.

ISBN: 978-1-9736-9704-6 (sc)
ISBN: 978-1-9736-9703-9 (e)

Print information available on the last page.

WestBow Press rev. date: 02/03/2021

CONTENTS

A special thanks goes out to Linda Gordon and William Brown for editing this book. Thanks also to my granddaughter, Erin, who helped with the book cover graphics. In addition, a very loving and heartfelt thanks goes to my wife Sue, who encouraged, supported, and kept me focused during this project. Without her, this book would not have been completed.

INTRODUCTION

Come, follow me, Jesus said, and I will
send you out to fish for people.
Mark 1:17 (NIV)

Why would anyone be called to lead a study on how
to witness, let alone write a book about it? As followers
of Christ, we are called to witness to people as Paul
did. But there are times when we may not know what
to say or do. I have heard so many times wonderful
Christians say that very thing: I just did not know
what to say or do.

This book is designed to discuss what it means to
plant seeds. It will cover some of the different ideologies
that may have an impact on what people believe or don't
believe. In addition, it will offer concepts and techniques
that will aid you in starting a conversation with someone.
It will also help in maintaining that conversation even if
it means just listening. It will also include ways to deal

with the different ideologies you may encounter. Lastly, there will be a chapter on how to help people in a hospice situation, how to deal with death of a loved one, and how to deal with a suicidal person.

CHAPTER 1

SOMETHING TO THINK ABOUT

[13]Blessed is the man who finds wisdom, the man who gains understanding, [14]for she is more profitable than silver and yields better returns than gold. [15]She is more precious than rubies; nothing you desire can compare with her. [16]Long life is in her right hand; in her left hand are riches and honor. [17]Her ways are pleasant ways, and all her paths are peace. [18]She is a tree of life to those who embrace her; those who lay hold of her will be blessed.
Proverbs 3:13-18 (NIV)

When you apply to become a counselor or therapist, the clinic you plan to work for will generally give you a personality test and ask a lot of personal questions about your view of things. The reason for this is to see if you have any feeling about certain people or issues that might influence your ability to help them. We Christians certainly have feelings and beliefs about certain types of behavior and issues, but as Christ teaches, we are to love all people no matter what they do or believe in.

This first chapter is designed to make you think about certain things that will hopefully help you look at situations differently. We will start with You just don't get it...... Some will be self-explanatory, others you may need a little help to understand. Here we go! "You just don't get it" ...

... when you say you love someone and then take them for granted.

... if you think sex and love are the same thing.

... if you don't vote and then complain about the government.

... when you complain about the farmers while you are at the dinner table eating.

... when you are FREE to criticize the military.

... if you believe the grass IS greener on the other side.

... if there is only one solution for EVERY problem. One thing you might have to do when helping someone is to help them find a new solution to a problem they are having.

... if you think plan A will always work and therefore you don't need a plan B.

... if you think TALKING ABOUT someone you are having a problem with will solve it. Think about it.

... if you try to teach the harmful effects of smoking with a cigarette in your mouth. Set the example; don't just teach it.

... if you think you can DEMAND respect. You can only earn it.

... if you think you are in control.

... if you believe YOU are the ONLY reason for your success.

... if you believe all experts ARE.

... if you think an excuse has an effective range greater than zero.

... if you think teaching your children "the facts of life" is the responsibility of the schools.

... if you believe every question only has one answer. Some do, some don't.

... if you think being late is fashionable.

... if you believe making a grand entrance makes you so.

... if you believe teaching your children is a job and not a commitment.

(I love this one) ... if you think commitment has a time limit.

Here are a couple for the guys out there.

... if you think you just don't get it means you are not getting any.

... if you think your job is to make the baby and her job is to take care of it.

Ladies here are a couple for you.

... if you believe the man you are staying with is YOUR life. If he is YOUR life, then you don't have one.

... if you believe the man you are staying with is SO SMART. So many times I would be working with ladies in the mental health clinic that were having relationship problems with the man they were staying with and I would hear the same thing any time I suggested they may want to consider taking a short break in the relationship - "but he's my LIFE and he's SO SMART". Need I say more.

Now back to everyone. Just a few more.

... if you believe marriage licenses are ownership papers.
... if you bring all your problems to God and forget to thank Him for the sunset.
... if you don't let God control your life.

How about some things you will surely miss.

You will surely miss something if you don't take time to rock a baby to sleep.
You will surely miss something if you never have a friend.
You will surely miss something if you don't take time to relax and do nothing.

You will surely miss something if you never
slow dance with someone you love.
And you will surely miss something if you
don't let God control your life.

I feel sure there are many more "You Just don't get it" and "You will surely miss something" that you can think of. You will have the chance when you go to the questions section of this book. These were just a few that I thought about over my time as a counselor and therapist. My students seemed to always enjoy them and they led to some good discussions.

There are a couple of additional thoughts I would like to share with you that I hope you will also think about. The Lord put on my heart, based on my counseling experience and by watching what is happening in the world, the following: Whatever man fears or does not understand, he will try to either dominate or destroy. This attempt at domination or destruction not only shows his weakness but exposes his low self-esteem and ignorance. Because of the above statement the following applies.

Where there is UNDERSTANDING AND PATIENCE-there is KNOWLEDGE.

Where there is KNOWLEDGE-there is SELF-ESTEEM.

Where there is SELF-ESTEEM-there is HONOR.

And where there is HONOR-there is UNDERSTANDING AND PATIENCE.

I leave you with this. It is what YOU believe in that creates a diverse world, or at least determines how you deal with it. Because of this fact, most people believe they are right even when they are wrong. SOOOOO!!! What we are dealing with here is THE HUMAN DILEMMA.

I hope this chapter gave you something to think about. Remember to let God help you when you witness.

------ C H A P T E R 2 ------

AN OVERVIEW OF WITNESSING

¹³Hold them in highest regard in love because
of their work. Live in peace with each other.
¹⁴And we urge you, brothers and sisters, warn
those who are idle and disruptive, encourage
the disheartened, help the weak, be patient with
everyone. ¹⁵Make sure that nobody pays back wrong
for wrong, but always strive to do what is good for
each other and for everyone else. ¹⁶Rejoice always,
¹⁷pray continually, give thanks in all circumstances;
for this is God's will for you in Christ Jesus.
1 Thess. 5: 13-17 (NIV)

When we think about witnessing as a Christian, we
think about spreading the word of God and telling
others of the total love and the price Jesus paid to save us
from our sins. As we will see in this book it is much more

than that. A witness, in legal terms, is someone who has direct knowledge of an event, usually by seeing it, or is an expert in the case that is being presented. Since we Christians were not present during the time Jesus walked on the earth, we need to be the experts when the case comes up for Jesus. We need to know about His life, His teaching, and His resurrection. How do we do that? Simple, we **ask** Jesus to come into our heart and we try to live by His teaching and actions. And how do we do that? We **accept** Jesus into our heart, become an expert by studying the Bible, and living in such a way that no one will doubt that we are Christians.

Since this book is about the art of witnessing, we need to start out by mentioning some key elements that you might want to be aware of in order to be an effective witness. These elements will have a direct impact on you and the person you are witnessing to. They are presented here in no particular order of importance.

SETTING: Where is the witnessing taking place - a church parking lot, funeral home, school or maybe in a line at a store? It could be under a tent manning a table to pass out material that invites people to have a closer relationship with the Lord. It could also be at your house or their house. The setting may not seem that important, but consider this, a church parking lot may be an easier place to witness than in a line at a store.

SITUATION: What event just happened? Was it a casual meeting? Was there a tragedy? The situation you find yourself in at the time you may be called on to witness will be extremely important.

STATE OF MIND: Is the person you may be witnessing to happy, sad, shaken-up, depressed, scared, or stressed? What they appear to be may not be what they are. It may be your task to find out just what state of mind they are in. Witnessing to someone who is scared is different than witnessing to someone who is shook up. Likewise, witnessing to a depressed person is different than a sad person.

RELATIONSHIP: What is the relationship of this person to you? Are they family member, co-worker, your boss, or your employee? Are they a member of your church or someone you just met? The relationship you have with the person you are witnessing to will be one of the most important factors that will determine how you witness to that person.

INVOLVEMENT: How did you get involved? Did you want to be involved? Were you asked to be involved? Did you feel the need to be involved? Was there a situation that you planned to be involved in? Were you forced to be involved? How you found yourself in a witnessing position will determine how you witness.

BELIEF STATUS: Are they a believer, non-believer, misguided believer, or are you unsure? This element goes without saying. The belief system of the person you are witnessing to will have a direct impact on how you witness. This will be covered in a later chapter.

WHAT DOES THE PERSON KNOW ABOUT YOU: Do you act like a Christian and they can tell (actions speak louder than words)? Do you talk like a Christian but not act like one (self-proclaimed)? Or do they know nothing about you? You can already see how this can affect the witnessing situation.

AGE AND SEX: This needs to be mentioned. In today's world the age and sex of the individual, the setting, and the situation you find yourself in has to be taken into account when witnessing. Be sure that the person you are witnessing to feels comfortable and safe.

Throughout this book you see how each one of these elements had a direct impact on just how successful your witnessing will be. Let's get started planting seeds.

---— CHAPTER 3 —---

PLANTING SEEDS

(You can't plant if you don't sow)

³Then he told them many things in parables, saying
"A farmer went out to sow his seed. ⁴ As he was
scattering the seed, some fell along the path, and the
birds ate it up. ⁵Some fell on rocky places, where it
did not have much soil. It sprang up quickly, because
the soil was shallow. ⁶But when the sun came up,
the plants were scorched, and they withered because
they had no root. ⁷Other seed fell among thorns,
which grew up and choked the plants. ⁸Still other
seed fell on good soil, where it produced a crop-a
hundred, sixty or thirty times what was sown"
Matthew 13:3-8 (NIV)

When we consider what a modern farmer does when
he plants his seeds, you can use the same principle for
planting Christian seeds, with one exception. A modern
farmer almost always has his field ready for his seeds to

go into good soil. Planting Christian seeds is like the sower in the scripture above. We do not always have good soil. In fact a lot of our seeds are sown on other-than-good soil because the Lord may speak to us or give us an opportunity to witness to those who might be considered not good soil. The good news is that the Lord can make the seeds sown on any path, rocky ground, or among thorns, bloom and blossom. We just need to get out there and sow.

Jesus did not sow seeds just on good soil. He is our example when it comes to sowing seeds. He witnessed to all sorts of people who could be considered the path, rocky ground and thorns. Remember Matthew 9:10-12 when Jesus was at Matthew's house having dinner with a group of sinners (which may not be considered good soil). The Pharisees ask the disciples what He was doing eating with the "like." [12]On hearing this, Jesus said "It is not the healthy who need a doctor but the sick." (NIV)

Also remember a woman caught in adultery (may not be considered good soil) who was brought to Jesus. John 8:3-11 tell us that the woman was brought to Jesus by the Teachers of the Law and the Pharisees. They had caught her in a sinful act. They informed Jesus that the penalty for such behavior was death by stoning. What did Jesus do? Bent down and doodled in the dirt. Of course the Teachers of the Law and the Pharisees keep on pushing (testing) Jesus. [7]When they kept on questioning him, he straightened up and said to them, "Let anyone who is without sin be the first to throw a stone at her." Then Jesus told her. ¹¹"Go now and leave your life of sin." (NIV)

Jesus had a problem with the Teachers of the Law and the Pharisees. He was always "calling them out" and/or "putting them in their place," as the above two situations demonstrate. As the result, most of the Teachers of the Law and the Pharisees left hating Jesus even more. The Bible does not tell us, however, just how many Teachers of the Law and Pharisees were touched by His actions on that day. There may have been many or only one who saw the love and compassion that Jesus had for this woman. We may never know how many lives we touch by just one act of kindness.

When we look back at the method that Jesus used to spread the word, we will notice that He dealt with people, not governments. He preached to people, not governments. He healed people, not governments. He forgave people, not governments. However, if one considers the Teachers of the Law and Pharisees a church-governing body, Jesus did get very angry with them. In Luke 11:46-52 we read;

> ⁴⁶Jesus replied, "And you experts in the law, woe to you because you load people down with burdens they can hardly carry, and you yourselves will not lift one finger to help them. ⁴⁷Woe to you, because you

build tombs for the prophets, and it was your ancestors who killed them. [48]So you testify that you approve of what your ancestors did; they killed the prophets, and you build their tombs. [49]Because of this, God in his wisdom said, 'I will send them prophets and apostles, some of whom they will kill and others they will persecute.' [50]Therefore this generation will be held responsible for the blood of all the prophets that has been shed since the beginning of the world, [51]from the blood of Able to the blood of Zechariah, who was killed between the altar and the sanctuary. Yes, I tell you, this generation will be held responsible for it all.[52]Woe to you experts in the law, because you have taken away the key of knowledge. You yourselves have not entered and you have hindered those who were entering." (NIV)

All these actions against the Teachers of the Law and the Pharisees that Jesus took only made these church leaders hate Him even more. So what did they do? They hung Him on a cross. It is one of the worst ways that man devised to execute someone. What did Jesus do while He hung on the cross? He asked His Father to forgive them.

As we witness, we must always use Jesus as an example. All of our witnessing should be done with love and patience. Do not judge. Have a firm knowledge of the Bible. Jesus knew the Law and He used it. Most importantly, always remember that Jesus will always be with you. Do not try and witness on your own. Call on Jesus and let Him guide you. He gave us the example (Himself) and the tools (the Bible and confidence) so that we might be successful. How we use them to plant seeds will be determined by who we are witnessing to. Do we have good soil or bad soil? It does not matter. The Lord can produce beauty in the worst places. We just have to plant the seeds.

NOT AGAINST FLESH AND BLOOD

¹²For our struggle is not against flesh and blood, but against the rulers, against the authorities, against the powers of this dark world and against the spiritual forces of evil in the heavenly realms. (EPH. 6:12 NIV)

Ephesians reminds us that our battle is not against man, but against rulers, authorities, powers of the dark world, and against spiritual forces of evil - in other words the beliefs of atheists, agnostics, and cults. In addition the concepts of non-believers and lukewarm Christians could be considered part of the spiritual forces of evil. The devil just loves non-believers and lukewarm Christians because he does not have to deal with them. The non-believer does not care and the lukewarm Christians believe they are on their way to heaven.

If a poll was taken as to which group would be the

most difficult to witness to, it would be interesting as to which one would come out on top. Actually, it does not matter. We witness to individuals not groups. Sure the beliefs of some groups are more anti-God than others, but we are still dealing with individuals. The strength of their commitment to their belief or concept would probably present the most challenge. Let us look at some of these groups.

NON-BELIEVERS

This group of people does not care and has nothing to do with Christianity or any other group. Sunday is just another day to them. Christmas is a time to receive cool gifts. They have no political agenda and could care less if a manger scene was on government property or private property. Merry Christmas or Happy Holidays greetings are not offensive to them one way or another. You certainly do not have to prove anything to them. They just go about their daily business. Whatever life throws at them, they deal with. It is not a big deal.

AGNOSTICS

One definition for an agnostic found on the internet states: "A person who believes that nothing is known or can be known of the existence or nature of God or anything beyond material phenomena. A person who claims neither faith in nor disbelief in God. We can see the difference right away between the non-believer and an agnostic. The agnostic needs proof of the existence of God." The non-believer could care less about existence of God or Jesus. On the surface, it looks like there is no hope for the agnostic. And, yes, we Christians cannot produce a material God or Jesus. But that does not mean they do not exist.

In his book Cold-Case Christianity, J. Warner Wallace uses his talent as a homicide detective to investigate the claims of the gospels. I believe you would find it relevant in your arsenal as you witness to the agnostic. J. Warner Wallace was an atheist by his own admission, before he started his detective investigation. He is now a wonderful believing Christian because of his findings.

Another tool to use is your own experience as it relates to your relationship with Jesus. The miracles that have happened in your life as the result of your belief in Christ and the miracles you have witnessed are great tools when witnessing to an agnostic. More on this wonderful, beautiful part of God's plan will be covered in a future lesson.

But here is the blessing Jesus has given us. In John 20:29 we find "Then Jesus told him (Thomas), 'Because you have seen me, you have believed, blessed are those who have not seen and yet have believed.'" (NIV) Jesus lets us know that there is no requirement for us to physically see Him or His father to be saved. But what we do see is the beautiful works of Jesus and His father in our everyday lives. We just have to recognize them.

LUKEWARM CHRISTIANS

Google lists an overwhelming number of definitions for a lukewarm Christian. From Christians who rarely attend church or read scripture but believe they are saved (once saved always saved) to those who attend church regularly and give regularly.

Let me explain. All those who had something to say about a lukewarm Christian had at least one thing in common, Revelations 3:15-16.

> [15]I know your deeds, that you are neither cold nor hot. I wish you were either one or the other. [16]So because you are lukewarm - neither hot or cold - I am about to spit you out of my mouth. (NIV)

Another scripture used, for example, was Matthew 12:30, which says "Whoever is not with me is against me, and whoever does not gather with me scatters." (NIV) Most of the other scriptures used concerning the lukewarm Christian were along the same lines. You are either for the Lord or against Him.

I have heard the term "once saved, always saved" all my life. My difficulty has been, as I grow as a Christian and my walk with the Lord becomes stronger, I find this statement not always true. You see the people I have heard this from rarely attend church, are not in tune with the scriptures and act more like non-believers than Christians. They believe they were saved at their baptism or they may have attended a revival where they accepted Jesus Christ as their Savior. But I guess they felt that was all they had to do. No follow up. No getting into the Word. Acting any way they want because the Lord will always forgive them, no repentance required. I don't need to <u>follow</u> Jesus because I am already saved.

The other extreme is the Lukewarm Christian who attends church regularly and gives regularly. They get involved in some of the church activities, but they seem to stay away from those activities that involve additional study and worship. They go about their daily activities and behave in such a way that is not Christ like. These are the Christians that give Christianity a bad name. What's sad is that there are some ministers and priests who fall into this type of Christian.

I had a client when I was working in a community mental health clinic who was the mistress of the minister of her church. She was referred to me because the director knew I was a Christian. We consulted scripture but she already knew what she needed to do. Her concern, besides the obvious, was her seeing the minister's wife sitting on the front pew shouting "hallelujah" as her husband talked about the perils of committing adultery. She repented and found another church, which was difficult for her because she had friends at that church. I do not know if she ever returned.

In the movie "War Room," Ms. Clara and Elizabeth,

Ms. Clara's real estate agent, sit down to discuss the asking price for Ms. Clara's house. Ms. Clara asks Elizabeth about her faith. Elizabeth gave the standard answer like "we attend church occasionally and pray at times." Ms. Clara asks if the minister of her church only preached occasionally. Ms. Clara then offered Elizabeth some coffee. When Elizabeth tasted the coffee, she asks Ms. Clara if she liked her coffee at room temperature. Ms. Clara said no, she liked her coffee nice and hot. Then Ms. Clara went on to explain about lukewarm Christians. So what is a lukewarm Christian? A short definition might be someone who knows about Christ but does not really KNOW Christ.

ATHEIST

The American Atheist's website quotes Madalyn Murry in the case of Murry vs. Curlett (1959) as saying the following regarding atheists:

> "Your petitioners are atheists, and they define their lifestyle as follows. An atheist loves himself and his fellow man instead of a God. An atheist accepts that heaven is something for which we should work for now – here on earth – for all men together to enjoy. An atheist accepts that he can get no help though prayer, but that he must

find in himself the inner conviction and strength to meet life, to grapple with it, to subdue it and enjoy it. An atheist accepts that only in a knowledge of himself and a knowledge of his fellow man can he find the understanding that will help lead to a life of fulfillment."

When I look at the above definition of an atheist I find I have more questions than answers about what an atheist is. For example what is their concept of God and heaven? What is their concept of prayer? Why do they feel they need to grapple and subdue life to enjoy it? But my main concern is their faith in man.

According to the book God's Not Dead and in the movie of the same name, most atheists were Christians at one time. Their faith was weak and when faced with a major tragedy and God did not answer their prayers concerning that tragedy the way they wanted, they turned against Him. I must admit I can understand how that can happen. Being a Christian is not always easy. When witnessing to an atheist, you may have to deal with not only their hatred of God but the tragedy that caused the hatred.

Another aspect of atheism is that it is a way of life. Atheists try and succeed at getting followers. Many colleges and universities have active atheist organizations. Their goal is to convince students that they do not need

God to succeed or be good. On the campus of the local community college on a table in the student center I found a pamphlet that said; {**"You can be GOOD without GODS!" Join ESSSA (the Enterprise State Secular Student Alliance, a student organization for atheists, agnostic, humanists, or any student without a religious or supernatural beliefs – a local affiliate of the national Secular Student Alliance.)**} As you can see this organization is part of a national organization.

Another big question to ask an atheist would be "Why do you feel you need to be part of an organization that excludes God to be good or successful?" Interesting! First of all, they need to understand that Christianity is not just about being good or successful. It is more than that. This could be a good starting point for witnessing.

CULTS

Why would anyone want to join a cult? Research tells us that the people who join a cult are searching for something and the cult they join provides that something. The leaders of cults are great con artists and know just what to say to that person who is searching. Jim Jones caused over 300 hundred people to take their lives willingly or by force with a gun put to their heads. Charles Manson had people murdered and his followers, who did the killing, in some cases, still believe it was the right thing to do because Charles said it was. This total control of the members is paramount for the cult to exist. There is no free will and total allegiance is required to remain a member, which is usually for life. Some of the methods used by cults border on torture. Sleep deprivation and withholding food, for example, may be used to keep members in line. Fear of death is also a common tool.

Another common characteristic of cults seems to be money. Almost all cults require you to give up almost everything you have and give it to the following. Brainwashing is the most common tool they use. They need you to believe in their way totally. Getting out of a cult is almost impossible. In some cults, you risk death, as stated above. The ones who do make it out are reluctant to say anything bad about their experience for fear of reprisal. When they do speak out they tell of the horror that goes on behind closed doors.

The sad thing about cults is that it is hard to witness to their members. They believe in the cult and that is that. During the Manson trial for the Tate and LaBianca murders, his followers (family) protested continuously outside the court house about the injustice being inflicted upon their leader. The family members who actually committed the murders felt no remorse for their actions because they believed they did the right thing because Manson said so. To this day, there are Manson family members who believe he is wonderful and feel he should be free because he is a great man and he did nothing wrong. Manson himself remained defiant and felt no remorse until his death in 2017.

From the above examples, it is easy to see just how difficult it can be to witness to a cult member. If the Lord provides the opportunity to witness to a cult member remember, the Lord will provide you with the words to plant a seed.

ROGUE CHRISTIANS

Of all the people you may find yourself witnessing to, the rogue Christian may be the most difficult. The impact rogue Christians have on Christianity is monumental. Numerous denominations have split because of the Rogue Christians. Rogue Christians are Christians who try to justify sinning. One of the most controversial issues today regards gays and lesbians. Denominations nationwide are endorsing gay and lesbian marriages. Others are ordaining gay and lesbian ministers. Sadly they try to use the Bible for this justification.

One argument the Rogue Christian uses is that Jesus never said it was wrong. He did not have to. It is made very clear in the Old Testament. Leviticus 20:13 says "If a man has sexual relations with a man as one does with a woman, both of them have done what is detestable. They are to be put to death; their blood will be on their own heads." (NIV) Paul also addressed this issue. We must remember that Paul had such a close relationship with Jesus, and he was filled with the Holy Spirit, that he spent his life preaching the teaching of Jesus. Jesus may not have mentioned homosexuality but his disciple Paul did. His writings were inspired by Jesus and he dealt with a lot of issues that Jesus did not mention. In 1 Timothy 1:8-11 we find:

> [8] We know that the law is good if one uses it properly. [9] We also know that the law is made not for the righteous but for the lawbreakers and rebels, the ungodly and sinful, the unholy and irreligious, for those who kill their fathers or mothers, for murderers,[10]for the sexually immoral, for those practicing homosexuality, for slave traders and liars and perjurers – and for whatever else is contrary to the sound doctrine [11]that conforms to the gospel concerning the glory of the blessed God, which he entrusted to me. (NIV)

The He Paul is referring to is, of course, Jesus. Another argument is that Jesus had a beloved disciple. Gays want you to believe that this disciple was Jesus' lover. That statement is not worth dealing with because it is so ridiculous.

I attended a Christian church that had all female ministers. That was acceptable because a lot of churches have female ministers. What was unorthodox was that their teaching and preaching was about mother god. They truly believed that God was a female. Their prayers always started with mother god. What else can be said?

These interpretations of the Bible are not biblical but are secular. Jesus addressed this very issue when He confronted the church leader of His time. We find in Mark 7:6-9 the following:

> [6]He replied "Isaiah was right when he prophesied about you hypocrites; as it is written: 'These people honor me with their lips, but their hearts are far from me. [7]They worship me in vain; their teaching are merely human rules.' [8]You have let go of the commands of God and are holding on the human traditions." [9]And he continued, "You have a fine way of setting aside the commands of God in order to observe your own traditions!" (NIV)

One other point you might want to consider when dealing with Rogue Christians is James' warning to the twelve tribes about worldly activities and beliefs. We find in James 4:4-6 these words:

[4]You adulterous people, don't you know that friendship with the world means enmity against God? Therefore

anyone who chooses to be a friend of the world becomes an enemy of God, [5]Or do you think Scripture says without reason that he jealously longs for the spirit he has caused to dwell in us? [6]But he gives us more grace. That is why scripture says: "God opposes the proud but shows favor to the humble." (NIV)

When dealing with Rogue Christians, you will need a strong knowledge of the Bible because that is what they use. Rogue Christians are tearing churches apart at an alarming rate. Thank God they are not tearing true Christians apart.

When you look at the overall situation that this chapter presents, it becomes obvious that there are those forces that want us not to follow the Christian life. Paul said it best in Colossians 2:8-10.

[8]See to it that no one takes you captive through hollow and deceptive philosophy, which depends on human tradition and elemental spiritual forces of this world, rather than on Christ. [9]For in Christ all the fullness of the Deity live in bodily form, [10]and in Christ you have been brought to fullness. He is the head over every power and authority. (NIV)

CHAPTER 5

PREPARING THE SOIL

> [5]Trust in the Lord with all your heart; do
> not depend on your own understanding.
> [6]Seek his will in all you do, and he will
> show you which path to take. [7]Don't be
> impressed with your own wisdom. Instead,
> fear the Lord and turn away from evil.
> Prov. 3:5-7 (NIV)

If a counselor begins a session with "What you need
to do is …" you might want to consider finding a new
counselor. Likewise, if you start to witness to someone
by saying; "If you don't repent of your sins you are
GOING TO HELL!!" you may find yourself with no
one to witness to. Most people I know do not like to be
told what to do or be threatened. This is certainly no
way to start a relationship.

When I worked as a therapist in a community
mental health center, most, if not all, of my clients liked

me. Believe me it was not because of my charming personality. It was because I established a relationship with my clients. Progress was made by us working together in dealing with the problems they were facing. The following DO'S and DON'T (guidelines) can help in establishing a relationship when witnessing.

DO....

.... listen and respond lovingly.
.... stay with the person you are witnessing to and sit quietly if necessary.
.... be genuine.
.... lead and guide.
.... use open ended questions.

DON'T....

.... push or pull
.... have the answers or solutions before you understand the questions or the problems.
.... say "I know how you feel"
.... ask "How did (does) that MAKE you feel."

Don't push or pull. Do lead and guide. Most people do not like being told what to do. Some people, however, don't mind because if the advice does not work out, they can blame the person giving the advice. Most people do not like being forced to do something either. Take the following example. You are trying to get a family to come to church, so you invite them to come. They say they will think about it. You start to tell them all the reasons they need to join you. You tell them that the sermons are great, the music is awesome, and the people are just wonderful. They very nicely repeat that they will think about it. You continue to say you will be willing to pick them up if they need a ride. What you do not know is that they had a very bad experience at the last church they attended. The church did not support them in a critical time of need. They felt neglected and alone when they reached out for help. You think what you are doing is what the Lord wants you to do by inviting non-church goers to church. You tell your Sunday school class that you are trying to get this family to come to church and the family keeps saying they will think about it. One of your Sunday school class members ask you "Why do you think they do not want to come?" You answer "I don't know." That may be the answer to the question. Hopefully, you have not made them angry by your persistence. Pushing or pulling is not the best way to influence people. Lead and guide. Establish a relationship. Which brings us to the next DO and DON'T.

Don't have the answers or solutions before you understand the questions or the problems. Do stay with the person you are witnessing to and sit quietly if necessary. A lot of people I know have their mind racing to come up with answers to their friend's questions even when they do not know the question or to have a solution before they know the problem.

In the example above, the family has a problem with churches. You are unaware of it because you were too busy pitching your church. You may want to take some time to see just where the family is when it comes to believing and church going.

Listening to the person you are witnessing to is very important as the following example points out. You are trying to comfort a friend who has just lost a loved one in a tragic accident. They are not a Christian but they are aware of God and Jesus. Your friend says "I just do not know why God would let this happen." Sound familiar? You respond by saying "If you just accept Jesus Christ as your Lord and Savior everything will be all right." That is not what your friend wants to hear. What they want is acknowledgment that you heard them. One way of letting them know is by repeating back to them what they had just said. A better response might be "I can understand why you might be wondering why God allowed the accident to happen." They might respond "Yeah!" At this point you have done three things. First you stayed where your friend was, second you established a relationship, and third you started a conversation that gives you an opportunity to witness. You might ask "Why do you feel that way?" This is an open ended question. It allows them to share their feeling and gives you better insight as to where they are in their belief system. If you were to ask "So you feel God let this happen?" You will get a yes answer and the conversation stops. Be prepared to handle some anger or answer a lot of questions, maybe both. Open ended questions require listening and responding to what they are saying. Saying "I know how you feel" is really an untrue statement. People say that all the time. Most of the time it may not get a response from the person you are saying it to but then again you may get a response you do not want, like "NO YOU DON'T!" The fact is you do not know how they feel. Some people believe that just because they had a similar situation happen in their lives, they have the right to say that.

Another question a lot of people ask is "How did (does) that MAKE you feel." It seems odd that this is even mentioned. When this was brought up in one of my counseling classes, I said to myself "you've got to be kidding." It was pointed out that people have choices as to how they feel. No one or nothing can make you feel a certain way. You chose how you are going to respond or feel. Yes it could be argued that the death of a child will MAKE you sad. Any normal person who has a loving spirit will feel sad. This should be a natural response. Getting angry as the result of the death of a child is much more of a choice. If the child dies as the result of an illness, that is one thing. But if the child dies suddenly and unexpectedly, that is something else. Both events will solicit feelings and what you do with those feelings is the important part. That is where the choice comes in. Understanding this concept will be a great help in witnessing. At this point you may be still confused by what I mean. Maybe with the exception of close family member or friends experiencing some sort of tragedy, people have a choice as to how they feel about any situation they may face. If you have a friend, for example, that did you an injustice and you say "He (or she) made me so mad." It was, believe it or not, your choice to get mad. I am not saying that it was a bad choice. What I am saying is that no one or situation can make you do or feel anything that you do not want to do or feel. You make that choice yourself. If someone dies after battling cancer for a long time I would hope you would choose to feel sad. But at the same time, you might also choose to feel happy and relieved because you know they are no longer suffering.

The last DO (guideline) is to be genuine. This can be hard to do if you are witnessing to someone who is continuing to do something that is against God's teaching. You don't like what your friend is doing and at the same time, you do not want to come across as judgmental. Let's say you have a friend, a member of your church, who is cheating on his wife (also a friend) and you want to confront him about it. Jesus tells us in Matthew 18:15 "If your brother or sister sins, go and point out their fault, just between the two of you. If they listen to you, you have won them over." (NIV) This can and will be very difficult. Being genuine means you must be honest about your feelings and concerns. Don't make your friend guess why you are talking to him. However, you don't want to start the conversation by saying, "Joe if you do not stop cheating on your wife, you are going to HELL!" This would certainly let Joe, know what you want to talk about. You might start out by saying, "Joe you may not think this is any of my business, but as your brother in Christ I am concerned about your extra marital activity." Wait for the response and be ready to deal with it in a loving and non-condescending manner. Let's face it, you are concerned, not only for Joe but for his family. In this example, however, Joe's wife is unaware of Joe's activity. That may have to be dealt with later. Joe may start giving all sorts of reasons why he is cheating, but the fact is none of them is valid. You may say you understand why HE thinks it's OK because of those reasons, but you inform him that it still does not make it right. All this time you are being honest and genuine. You are also being a good friend.

This brings me to the last and maybe the most important guideline. It is not listed in the do's or don'ts because it stands alone. NEVER GIVE UP! Jesus does not give up on us and we certainly do not want to give up on those people we have witnessed to (planted a seed). If the opportunity to follow up in person is offered, take it. If not, continue to go to the Lord in prayer

—————— CHAPTER 6 ——————

THE ART OF WITNESSING

> [8] But you will receive power when the Holy Spirt
> comes on you; and you will be my witnesses in
> Jerusalem, and in all Judea and Samaria, and
> to the ends of the earth. Acts 1:8 (NIV)

In this chapter we will explore ways to witness to the
people mentioned in chapter two. I will offer suggestions
and present examples that may help you plant seeds. The
key word here is suggestions. Let us look at some ways
to plant seeds.

Witnessing to a non-believer is not that difficult. It
may take a lot of love and patience, however. Actions will
speak louder than words in most cases. Family members,
good friends, co-workers and other non-believers are for
the most part, very good people. The problem is they
are not saved and that can hurt your heart. You want
them to experience the love Jesus has for them. You also
want them to be in heaven with you. You understand

John 14:6 ⁶Jesus answered, "I am the way and the truth and the life. No one comes to the Father except through me." (NIV)

How you treat the non-believer is very important. Taking that little extra step to make their life a little easier goes a long way. Remember, they already know you are a Christian so act like one. As a Christian, your lifestyle revolves around the church and its activities. Invite them to be a part of that life. Invite them to the Easter play that your child is in. Have them join you to hear the Christmas cantata. Bring them along when you go to a church rummage sale. Help them enroll their children in a VBS or Winshape (a program put on in the summer for children sponsored by Chick Fil-A). Invite them to help you deliver food to the homebound. Can you see where I am going with this? Christian fellowship with a non-believer may open up opportunities for verbal witnessing. They make a comment about how much their child enjoyed the church activity they were involved in. That comment may be the start of a great spirit filled conversation. The Lord can work wonders when the door is opened. Let me share an experience my wife and I had.

We volunteered our services to help with the youth program in a church in Tennessee. We were stationed at Fort Campbell at the time and ended up being the Junior High counselors. We wanted to have an all-day planning session to plan for the coming year's activities. We asked the youth members if they would ask their parents if we could use their homes to plan the different types of activities we were going to participate in. We needed four homes and we got four homes. We ate breakfast at the first home and planned our programs. We had lunch at the second home and planned our church related projects. At the third home we had dinner and planned our community service projects. At the fourth home we had our dessert and planned our outings such as movie night or a water park. The idea of going to the youths' homes was to get the parents involved. In one of the homes we went to only the youth member attended church. The parents did not. I mentioned to the dad just how much we appreciated them letting us use their home to plan our activities. I also let him know just how much we enjoyed having his son being part of our youth group. I pointed out just how much he added to the youth group, and what a great example he was to others. The next Sunday his parents started coming to our church.

Agnostics need proof that God exits. Let them help you provide that proof. Don't give them an example of God's work and then explain it to them. Take the other approach. Share with them an experience you or someone else had that only God could have provided the outcome. A word of caution: don't give a healing experience as your proof. Most agnostics and some doctors, who have witnessed the healing power of Jesus, will give science the credit.

Generally speaking, most agnostics will not shy away from a good conversation about God or Jesus. Unlike atheists they are not trying to change your mind about God or Jesus, they just want the proof that they exist. When you think about it, they are seekers so help them find the truth. Here is one experience I had while working with Hospice as a social worker. I would like an agnostic to explain to me how it happened without God's hand involved.

I was called to a patient's home one Sunday afternoon. The husband of the patient was having difficulty with his wife being near death. When I arrived there were a lot of friends and family already there. One of the friends was a nurse so when I asked if they wanted one of our nurses to come and help with their mother, they said no their friend would help. The patient was in what we (hospice workers) considered to be in a death coma. Patients can be in the death coma for days. At other times it could be minutes. The point is no one knows when a person is going to die. At one point I found myself standing on one side of the patient's hospital bed with her husband on the other. He said, "George how much longer do you think she will live?" I said without hesitation, "She will leave us within three hours." I immediately said to myself, "Are you crazy? You don't know that!" But then there was an instant peace that overcame me. I smiled to myself because I knew who was in control. It gets even better. Later, I was in the kitchen with the patient's children. I asked, "Who is not here? Your mom is waiting for someone." This is not an unusual question because we can, to some extent, tell when a patient is holding on. The answer was that one of the brothers was coming in from out of town and he was expected at any time. I told them that when he arrived, they should gather the friends and family members who they wanted to be with their mom when she passes. I further said, "She will not be with us fifteen minutes after he gets here." Once again, I could not believe what I had just said. The peace came to me once again. I told the family I would usher the other people out of the room so they could have some private time with their mom. The brother arrived and I went outside to be with some of the friends who were there. One person lit up a cigarette, smoked it rather rapidly and started to smoke another one. About that time, the family called me to come in and the nurse informed me she had just passed. The reason I mentioned the cigarette smoking, was that it let me know about how much time had passed from the time the son arrived to when his mom died. I understand that it takes a person 5 to 10 minutes to smoke a cigarette. Based upon the time that the first cigarette was smoked and the lighting up of the other, I figured 10 to 15 minutes had passed since the son had arrived and his mother's death. I left my home about 1 pm and arrived at the patient's house 15 minutes later. I got back to my house around 3:30 pm. The patient died well within the three hours the Lord had predicted. One of the cool things about this experience, besides the obvious, was at no time did I feel the need to check my watch. The Lord was in control and only by looking back at the situation did I determine the time frames. You will be exposed to more wonderful experiences in the chapter "Wow! You're Good."

When dealing with the Lukewarm Christian one must take more of an educational approach. Lukewarm Christians already know about God and Jesus but, as stated in chapter two, they don't know God and Jesus. Witnessing to them involves more of a teaching approach and refreshing their memory about the love and grace of Jesus and accepting Him as their Lord and savior.

Many people believe "Once saved, always saved." They live their lives like I can do anything I want and all I have to do is ask for forgiveness and all will be good. They seem to forget the repent part about asking for forgiveness. They seem to forget that they need Jesus in their lives to guide and comfort them at all time. If the Lord has laid upon your heart to witness to someone and during the conversation you ask them, "Are you saved?" and they say, "Yep!" you may take this opportunity to have them tell you about their conversion experience. Some will say, I grew up in the church. Others will give you a date, time, and place. After you receive the answer, you might ask "So how has your life changed since your acceptance of Christ?" Go from there.

Atheists will be a handful. The one saving grace is they have no problem talking about God, heaven, prayer and other Christian beliefs. You just have to be prepared to deal with their nonsense. I am sorry to say, but you may have to fight fire with fire. Quoting the Bible here will not work as easily as you might think. Your defense may have to come from other atheists who have found the Lord and are happy to tell about it in their books. As I stated earlier one such person is J. Warner Wallace, (Cold Case Christianity). He offers proof of the existence of Jesus. He started his research trying to disprove God's existence and power and ended up believing. The movies "God's Not Dead" and "God's Not Dead 2" present wonderful arguments as to the existence of God and Jesus. Rice Broocks, author of the books God's Not Dead and Man Myth Messiah gives compelling evidence as to the existence of Jesus. He pulls from all types of resources, both secular and Christian to give the facts about Jesus. As I also said earlier I would suggest reading the books or watching the movies. They will have an impact on your life and provide you facts about the life and times of Jesus.

Atheists have to be dealt with on their own battlefield. The Lord has already provided you your sword (Bible) and He will be with you in the fight.

Cult members are rarely seen. Most cults are very secret and if they are out there in the public, such as the Scientologist, the only way to really know what they are like is to be a member. The people who are able to get out have a lot of trouble getting other family members out. They do share stories of what happens inside that cult. The most common practice is brainwashing. Making people believe that giving up everything and giving any additional money to the cult will give them the peace and hope they are looking for. The leaders live in luxury while the members live in poverty. Sure, there are some famous people who are part of the Scientology cult. Some other famous people have left and told stories of the horror that goes on in that cult.

So how do you witness to cult members? You witness the same way you would witness to any nonbeliever. However, you have to know what you are up against. This can be very difficult. You may have to do research on what the cult is all about and what they are offering. Then you need to make them a better offer that allows REAL peace and joy that only requires accepting Jesus. No money or sacrifice. Jesus already did that for us.

Rogue Christians will be the greatest challenge because they truly believe they are right. You can try and point out where they are bending the rules and they will try to point where they are not. You will have to have a very strong Biblical background. You will also have to believe in the word of God as it is presented in the Bible. If it says "Thou shalt not" it means do not do it. If it says certain behaviors are wrong, they are. These need to be pointed out and stood behind. When witnessing to a Rogue Christian, someone in that conversation needs to stand up, keep the FAITH and remain true to the WORD OF GOD. That is what it is all about. WHAT DOES THE BIBLE SAY ABOUT IT?

If you are a member of a Rogue church, you must remain strong in your faith. Your witnessing must be, as with all witnessing, Bible based. You must continue to point out, in a loving way, that the path your church is on can lead to destruction. If you feel that your witnessing is not producing fruit, you may find yourself needing to go somewhere else to worship.

Your church is your family. Paul lets us know this when he writes to the Christians in Corinth by saying; "Finally, brothers and sisters, rejoice! Strive for full restoration, encourage one another, be of one mind, live in peace. And the God of love and peace will be with you." 2 Corinthians 13:11 (NIV) Our church family are our brothers and sisters. When a member is hurting, we must provide them comfort. When they are in need, we must try to help with that need. When they are lonely, we must include them. Many large churches have paid ministers to provide these services. If you are member of such a church, you are not excused from helping in those areas just because you have a minister to do it. Bring comfort to the sick. Visit those in prisons. Help those in need. Encourage one another and be of one mind. Don't leave it just to the ministers of your church.

At times you may be called on to witness to a church member. Once again, be kind and gentle. The Lord will help you in these situations. This can and often is very difficult to do.

Witnessing to members of your own family, weather they are biological, adopted, or blended, can be one of the most difficult things to do. Why? Because there is such an emotional aspect inherent with this type of witnessing. Your family may be dysfunctional or normal (whatever that means). No matter what type of family you have, there should always be the feeling of togetherness and love. At this point I could write another book on how to deal with dysfunctional families. I don't need to because there are already many books on the subject. All I want to suggest is for you to search your heart when dealing with family members who are unchurched, on drugs, or otherwise living an alternate life style that not in keeping with the teaching of Jesus. We have members in my church, as in other churches, who have relatives who are dealing with substance abuse or are gay. They hurt for their family members. Sometimes the only thing you can do is take it to the Lord in payer. Never give up.

How you witness to others depends on who you are witnessing to and the circumstances in which the witnessing will take place. You may not have the opportunity to talk about Christ at first or maybe not at all. Actions may speak louder than words. Remember, you are planting the seed. The Lord will then take over. Be aware, He may continue to include you in the nurturing of that seed.

CHAPTER 7

WITNESSING IN DIFFICULT SITUATIONS

³⁴Jesus said. "Father forgive them, for they know
not what they are doing." And they divided up
his clothes by casting lots. Luke 23:34 (NIV)

The above scripture tells about Jesus witnessing while hanging on the cross. Hanging on a cross could be considered a difficult situation to witness, but Jesus did. Trying to witness to someone who has just lost a loved one in a horrific accident might be considered a difficult situation to witness. Dealing with someone wanting to kill themselves certainly is a difficult situation to witness in.

Why did God let this happen? Good question. Let us look at some ways we might handle that question. First we need to address the basic question. Did God in fact let this happen or was it the circumstances surrounding the tragedy. We could also ask the following questions: Did God let the man go to the bar and drink with his buddies or did he choose to? Did God let him get drunk, or did he choose to? Did God let him get behind the wheel, or did he choose to? Did God let him drive across the center line, hit a car killing all on board, and walk away without a scratch? Or did God try and prevent this tragedy? DON'T DRINK AND DRIVE is posted on big billboards. DRINK RESPONSIBLY is stated by alcohol manufacturers at the end of all their commercials. State troopers put public services messages out all the time on TV about drunk driving. Organizations such as MADD (Mother Against Drunk Driving) are also putting out public service messages. What more can God do? When you really look at a lot of these horrible tragedies, most of them are the result of choices **people** have made. In many cases, those choices impact the lives of others.

Let's look at another circumstance and ask a different question. The parent is in the house and the child asks to go outside and ride her bike. The parent says just a minute and then tells her to put on her helmet and get her bike out. The parent then goes outside to watch her daughter ride her bike. She enjoys watching her. She tells her daughter to stay on the sidewalk. The little girl says OK and heads out. She is riding on the sidewalk and a puppy runs out in front of her. She swerves to miss the puppy, and jackknifes the front wheel of her bike causing her to flip over the handlebars. She hits her head and breaks her arm. The bike landed on her legs and breaks both of them. This injury will result in the child having difficulty walking for the rest of her life. Why did the parent let this happen? Could the parent have prevented this accident? The answer is yes. The parent could have kept her in and not let her go outside and play. The parent did not have to buy her a bike. The point is, we all make choices. The parent chooses to let the child ride her bike. The child chooses to not hit the puppy. Both are good choices but the results of those choices did not end well.

Now God could treat us the same way. He could take away all free will. He could make all the choices for us. In other words He could run our lives and then we would not have to do anything but be a total robot for Him. He could be a very stern father who demands and forces all of His children to worship Him or die. God started out and continues to love us much more that we deserve. He does everything He can to protect us. He lets us make our own choices and live our own lives. He will guide us and care for us even when we do not ask Him. All He asks from us is to accept His son, whom He sacrificed for our sins, and live by His example.

God does not want any of His children hurt or killed. Instead He gives us choices. He is patient and kind. He hurts when any of His children are suffering. And, sad to say, He has been pushed aside. He is not wanted in our schools, and our government is doing everything it can to get Him out of America. It does not take much to notice what is happening in America today with all the shootings in schools and other facilities. The answer is to take away the guns from innocent people and their Bibles also. Don't let guns (good plan) or Bibles (bad plan) in our public school system. We sure don't want prayer either. Don't let goodness and truth be taught to our children. Let's just ask, "Why did God let this happen?" Let's blame Him.

Now the real question is how do I answer the question? First, you need to understand the situation that the person is in. Second and foremost, you must provide comfort and concern. Your initial answer should be I don't know, because you don't. You must help the person work through their grief. Much later you might have the opportunity to suggest that God may not have let it happen. It was the circumstances. You might want to inform them that God is hurting also, because He is.

Another difficult situation is dealing with a suicidal person. First and foremost, stay with the person who wants to take his life. Do not let him be alone.

Now, how do we handle the situation? First you need to determine if the person you are with wants to kill himself. This can be difficult. Telling you that you have been a good friend, saying all my problems will be solved very soon, feeling very good all of a sudden after they have been very depressed, are all signs that the person is thinking about or had made a decision about killing himself.

If a friend, co-worker, church member, or anyone for that matter, starts to act in certain ways after being depressed for a long time or had a tragedy happen in their life, you may want to take notice. The examples given in the above paragraph are warning signs of the possible consideration of taking one's life.

Let us look at two different situations you may find yourself in when dealing with a possible suicidal person. Both situations must be dealt with differently. In the first situation you suspect that someone you know may want to kill himself. You need to approach him in a private setting. If it is someone who works for you, you may want to call him into your office. If it is a friend, you may want to invite him over or go visit him. Keep it private.

Now at this point, I could write another book on how to handle suicidal people. So what I plan to do is hit some highlights you might want to consider when faced with the above situation. The privacy will allow you to speak frankly about your concerns. Establish a relationship and explore how the person is doing. If the response is fine, have the person give you their definition of fine. Remember the reason you are talking with them is because everything does not appear fine to you. You have noticed some behavioral changes that are not consistence with the person's, what I call, normal life pattern. A normal life pattern is a phase I use to describe how an individual deals with everyday life circumstances. How they deal with a crisis, for example. Some people may withdraw so they can process the situation and then respond. Others may get very active immediately because they feel they have to do something about the situation now. Still others may display a lot of anger. No matter how the person responds, if it is normal for them, then there may be nothing to worry about. If they do not respond in their normal life pattern, then there may be some concern. Let us look at two situations that might cause some concern about an individual behavior.

Your friend has been having a lot of life problems. He can't maintain work because he is always being laid off due to the economy. His wife is starting to feel the pressure and is threatening to leave him. His dad, who just happened to be one of his support systems, was killed in an auto accident not too long ago. He comes to you to talk because his wife has just left him and took the kids. He starts out the conversation by informing you of his wife's departure. He is very calm about it and seems to understand her actions. This is not the friend you are familiar with. He is usually very active in dealing with pressure. He always gets up when knocked down. Now he is calm and he tells you that everything is fine and he has everything worked out. He goes on and lets you know just how much of a good friend you have been. What do you do? What question might you ask?

An employee who works for you has been depressed for some time. You have spoken with him and you feel comfortable that he is handling his situation, based on what you know about his normal life pattern. One day he shows up for work all happy and is acting like he has not a care in the world. You talk with him to find out why the change. He tells you he has found a solution to his problems. Everything is fine and no one has to worry about him anymore. Is there a concern here? What will be your next response?

These are two examples of people who might be considering killing themselves. Your question might be "What has happened to make you feel this way?" Expect an answer that will appear to be positive and designed to throw you off of their intentions. Something like, "Oh I decided to take the bull by the horns and deal with it." "Well good for you!" should not be your next response. You need to find out, in both cases, what exactly their plans are to solve the problems they have been dealing with. The more they try to dodge the questions about their plans, the more concerned you should be.

Two key phrases in the above examples give you a clear clue as to their thought processes. In the first example saying you HAVE been a good friend lets you know that they are planning to go somewhere. Where? In the second example saying that "no one has to worry about me anymore" lets you know that whatever he has planned is going to cause people not to be concerned about him. What is the plan?

Staying with the person is the most important thing you can do. Continuing to ask open ended questions about the person's plans gives you better insight as to what is going on with this person. If they continue to "beat around the bush" you may have to confront them about what you are thinking. One way to do this is to make a statement such as, "By what you have been saying (or not saying) one might think you might be planning to kill yourself." Expect a reaction. One might be anger while another might be silence, or something in between. At any rate be ready to explain why you feel that way.

If it is anger, it could be something like, "Are you crazy!" or "I can't believe you said that. What kind of a friend are you?" These reactions do not necessarily mean that the person is not going to kill themselves. They once again are designed to throw you off. These answers could also be designed to get you mad at them. You getting mad at them gives them another reason to believe they are worthless. "Even my best friend hates me. No one loves me." As stated above, you may need to explain how you reached that conclusion.

If they give you the silent treatment you might say, "By your silence, I am right, aren't I?" Notice the person's behaviors and look at their eyes. You may be surprised at what you see. One thing I have noticed about suicidal people, they seemed to be relieved once their intentions are found out. This relief is usually because someone has recognized just how badly they feel. That someone (you) might be able to help them or get them help. One note here, if someone is hell bent on killing themselves, they will do it. Intervention is almost impossible if not impossible. They will give very little if any indication of their intentions. They do not want to be stopped. They want to die.

Once you have discovered your friend or employee may want to harm themselves, don't try and talk them out of it. Telling them everything will be all right tomorrow or saying "How do you think your (put relationship of the person here) will feel if you do this?" might just strengthen their conviction. They really don't care how anyone feels. You first must acknowledge their feelings. Saying something like, "You must be really hurting to consider killing yourself." or "Can you help me understand why you are considering killing yourself?" Get them talking and listen. Be supportive, not of their plan of course, but of them.

They own the total conversation. If they are quiet you are quiet. At one point, after a long silence, you might ask "What are you feeling now?" or "What are you thinking?"

Two facts you must consider when dealing with a suicidal person: First as long as they are with you what are they not? DEAD! Second you need to try to insure their safety. How do you do this? First and foremost, realize that you are dealing with a person who wants to kill themselves. Therefore be ready to take the necessary measures to protect them from themselves. You may have to involve the police. If you can get them to share with you someone they trust (it might be you) to take care of them, call that person and tell them the situation and have them come over. Inform them that this person needs to be put in a hospital if at all possible for further help. Once that friend or family member has taken charge of the person, they become responsible for that person. If you are that person they trust, you need to find a way to get your friend to a hospital. This can be tricky. It may involve the police. Saving one's life is what is important here. If the police are involved, they will be more than happy to assist. They will escort your friend (or family member) to the medical facility. They and the hospital can help you go through proper procedures to insure that the person is taken care of. Once the police have the person in their custody, they become responsible for the person. Once the hospital has the person, they are now responsible for the person. You have saved a life. What a great way to witness.

I must emphasize two major points. First, the above suggestions on what to say are only suggestions. The actual situation you find yourself in will dictate your comments. The message here is to be gentle, quiet if necessary, understanding, supportive, and patient.

Remember the person you are dealing with owns the conversation. The second is drastic measures may need to be taken to save the person's life. Don't hesitate to take them if necessary.

A lot of people want to take the blame when a family member or close friend kills themselves. I had clients who had to deal with a suicide. In many cases, the person who killed him or herself, made the family member or friend feel guilty about what happened. They start the conversation with something like; "If only I would have done (whatever) he (she) would not have killed themselves." At that point in time, I would have to help them to understand that it was the choice the person made to take their own life. There are times when suicide may have been a mistake. A person choosing a slow method to die may be reaching out for help. The problem is they were not discovered in the time the victim was hoping for and the result is the death of the individual. Or the method chosen was too lethal, like taking too many pills, for example.

No matter how the person took their life, **THEY MADE THE DECISION.** Helping a family member or friend deal with the guilt is very difficult. At those times, it is best to be very supportive and help them understand about choices. Expect a lot of what ifs or I should haves. In these cases, it might be better to suggest that the person seek professional help. Do it with love.

Christians should never be afraid of witnessing in

difficult situations. The Lord is behind us and we are His tools to help those people who find themselves in a place that no one likes to be in. Be patient and listen. And above all NEVER GIVE UP.

CHAPTER 8

WOW! YOU'RE GOOD

⁷Jesus said to the servants, "Fill the jars with water,"
so they filled them to the brim. ⁸Then he told them,
"Now draw some out and take it to the master of
the banquet." They did so, ⁹and the master of the
banquet tasted the water that had been turned into
wine. He did not realize where it had come from,
though the servants who had drawn the water knew.
Then he called the bridegroom aside and said,
"Everyone brings out the choice wine first and then
the cheaper wine after the guests have had too much
to drink; but you have saved the best till now." ¹¹What
Jesus did here in Cana of Galilee was the first of
the signs through which he revealed his glory, and
his disciples believed in him. John 2:7-11 (NIV)

This was the first miracle recorded that Jesus did. He
is still doing them today. The following are modern
miracles experienced by different people who worship

and love the Lord. They are in their own words. I guess, when you think about it, they could be used to help when witnessing.

I was told by the nurses that one of my patients (42 years old) had received some disturbing news from her doctor. Her doctor informed her, through her brother, that her kidneys were failing and she may not make it through the weekend. You must understand that this lady was not even close to death. She was very mobile and looked as healthy as anyone I had seen. She had cancer and it was inoperable. When I arrived at the patient's home that Friday morning, the house was already full of friends and relatives. I went in and found the patient sitting on the couch. I noticed a little space beside her, so I squeezed in. I started the conversation by saying, "Hey! I heard you have received some news about your condition." She told me what the doctor had said. I then told her that I wanted to say hi to her parents and that if I did not get another chance to talk with her again, I would see her on Monday. About 20 minutes later the nurses showed up to see how she was doing. About 10 minutes later they called me into the bedroom to talk with the patient. The patient asked me what I meant by telling her I would talk with her on Monday. Based upon what the doctor had told her she thought that may not be possible. I said I had no doubt about her being around Monday and beyond. Then I told her she had a bigger problem than what the doctor had told her. She and the nurses looked at me like I had three heads. I asked her how she was handling all the people coming up and telling her how sorry they were about her news. She said it was difficult because of all the sadness. I told her the next time someone said they were sorry, ask them why. And then follow it up by saying, "If I die, I will be with the Lord. And if I don't I will be with my family and friends. I win both ways." She started crying and the nurses started crying. I looked up and said to the Lord "Wow! You're good!" The patient lived two more months. Need I say more?

In another hospice situation, I was told by one of our hospice nurses to run by, and do an intake of one of our new patients. According to the nurse, she was alert and seemed to be doing well. The nurse also informed me that the patient's home had a bug problem, so I made some phone calls to see if I could get the problem resolved. I also contacted DHR (Department of Human Resources) because the patient had two small children that might need to be taken care of. The patient had a 21 year old son but he was unable to take care of his younger sisters. The patient had a boyfriend but he too was unable to care for the children.

When I arrived at the patient's home, it was apparent the nurse was right about the bug problem. I also noticed that the patient was in her death coma. I looked up and said, "I am not leaving until this is over, am I?" I almost felt God smiling when He told me "NO!" The next thing

I noticed was the area around patient's bed was clean and nice. It was like none of the bugs or any other trash or debris was going to touch this lady. I proceeded with doing the intake with the 21 year old son. At one point I noticed I was the only other grown up besides the son and his girlfriend. I told him he needed to start calling some of the family and friends because his mother was near death. The family and friends started to arrive. Also the DHR person came by. In addition the bug people dropped in. They informed me that the bug problem could be handled but that, between the two of them, they had not seen such a bad infestation in their careers. I told them, I did not believe they would be needed.

And now for the miracle, I was on the porch finishing up my intake when the two girls, one ten and the other twelve, rushed out and said, "Mr. George! Mr. George, mommy is awake and you can talk to her now." I looked up and said, "It's time isn't it?" He said, "Yes" I went in and the first thing I noticed was how radiant the patient was. Her eyes were clear and focused. It reminds me of Psalm 34:5 "Those who look to him are radiant; their faces are never covered with shame." (NIV) The girls were yelling, "Mommy, mommy Mr. George is here." I told them that their mommy could not hear them because she was looking at Jesus and was going to be with Him right now. The patient closed her eyes, smiled, tilted her head to the left and let her last breath out slowly. All I could think of was WOW what a wonderful death. This lady is surely with the Lord.

I've got one more. I can't help it. I love sharing these wonderful encounters with the Lord I have been so blessed to be a part of.

I stopped by one of my patients that I just loved to visit. She was a lovely elderly lady. I loved being around her just to listen to her stories about the "good old days." She always had on her Christian music and we would just talk. I also loved her hugs I would receive when I would leave. This particular visit I noticed she looked like someone had put makeup on her face. It was just right and made her look radiant (sound familiar). I talked with her for a time, got my hug, and went to say good-bye to her children. I asked who had put the makeup on my patient. They responded no one had. I knew the patient was unable to put it on herself. I told them just how wonderful she looked. I said good-bye and on the way out of the house I told the Lord that I believed I would not see her again. Then I asked, "Will I?" He answered "No you will not." She went to be with Him during the night.

~ ~ ~

Gordon is a member of the church I attend. He is also a member of the Christian Motorcycle Association. Even though it is not required to own a motorcycle to be in this organization, it is a plus to have one. Gordon is very active in this organization and puts many miles on his cycle. The following is his testimony about his motorcycle accident.

I had my motorcycle for 14 years and had ridden it 114,000 miles. I was starting to get the wanderlust for a new motorcycle in 2012. I am getting older and had shoulder issues so instead of a new bike, my wife suggested I just get a better fitting handlebar. Instead of telling her the bars were 15,500 I made the mistake of telling her the bars were 150, when she asked. Two years later while serving a ministry opportunity in the local Harley shop I was just mesmerized by one of the bikes. It was like a light beam from heaven (actually well placed xenon showroom lights) made me really want to trade right then and there. Again my wife intervened and asked what would make the old Valkyrie more comfortable- a new Corbin seat- which she bought me for Christmas. I had had some other service issues with the bike and had one bike shop do some major suspension repairs. After those repairs, the bike was just not handling correctly and after one ride slowly driving the bike into my garage the front wheel locked up and left a skid mark on the floor. I knew something wasn't right.

I went to another bike shop and had a long conversation with the service manager about my concerns with the bike. We made arrangements for an appointment to do some major service work. I put the new seat on the bike

I had gotten for Christmas and on January 6th rode the bike to the bike shop. It was late afternoon and mild rush hour traffic. I had made arrangements for my wife to meet me at the shop and then we'd go out to eat.

As I approached the intersection where I would turn right to head to the bike shop, I saw ahead of me several cars were slamming on their brakes and there were several rear-ending each other. I avoided hitting the car in front of me and as I applied the brakes the front wheel locked up like I was on ice. Faster than the snap of a finger (I don't know who has those slow motion experiences) I was thrown to the ground like someone had taken me by the feet and slammed me to the ground. Before I hit the ground I had a conversation, actually more like a short question, "Is this how you'll take me?" There was an almost angry "No" answer. By the time I had hit the ground the helmet had broken my collar bone and first rib and the impact landing on my left arm broke ribs 2-9. It hurt like a big dog. Then I felt like I was being rolled and had to roll on those broken ribs 3 times! I was well aware of that and remember putting my right foot out to stop my rolling but was out of control. By this time other traffic behind me and I need to crawl across the road to get to the shoulder and all I can do is affirm my love for my Jesus. I am a little short of breath at this time as my left lung has collapsed from the rib fractures, but manage to lay on my right side, retrieve my flip phone, and without my reading glasses find my wife's number to have the first responder call my wife and have her meet me at the ER. There was an air of anger about me that was almost palpable, at the instant of the accident, that dissipated as I was crawling across the road. I believe this was the Evil One. I would find out the next day my brother-in-law was killed in a car accident about an hour and a half after mine. I don't know if he was angry he couldn't have the both of us in one day. I was so thankful my mother didn't get two death notices the same night.

Within three months of the accident I did in fact buy that Harley I had seen in the store a year before the accident.

~ ~ ~

C.T., another member of my church, was telling a fellow member of our church how the Lord has given him his sight back. I asked him if he would mind telling me his story and letting me put it in this book. This is his story.

In my late seventies (I am much older now), I had cataract surgery done in both eyes. At first I had no problem with the surgery or my eyes. While I was on a trip to a town in north Alabama, I can't remember the name of it at this time, I started losing sight in my right eye. By the time I reach my destination, I had lost all vision in that eye. At first I thought something has gone wrong with the cataract surgery. This was on a Friday. I returned to Enterprise. Being a weekend there wasn't an ophthalmologist available. I had to wait till Monday to see a local ophthalmologist. She told me I had a torn retina. She sent me immediately to a specialist in Dothan. He examined me and told me my retina was completely detached. He then started treatment right away. The first thing I had to do was to sit still with my head back for 24 hours. It was a terrible situation. He then started a series of operations that went on for several weeks. The operations restored my sight to where I could at least see light. He then let me know that I would probably not get my sight totally back. There was a small section of the retina that he was unable to reattach. He set up the next appointment, which was going to be the last one, for the following day. The operation was either going to fix it or not. That night, around eight o'clock, I was heading for the bathroom. When I reached the door to go in, I felt a sort of twitching sensation in my right eye. Immediately my vision was restored to what I would say 90 percent, maybe more. When I went to the doctor that next day, he continued to look and look in my eye. I said to him, "It's healed isn't it." He said, "To my surprise it is. The retina is completely reattached." I told him that the Lord did it. He then said, "That is a wonderful thing He did." I said, "Yes, and praise the Lord."

Either Gordon's, C.T.'s or my experiences were the result of devine intervention, or we fabricated them.

We were just as shocked at these occurrences as anyone who might have witnessed them. Gordon, C.T. and I believe that our God was present in the situations and we welcome anyone to try and explain them otherwise.

~ ~ ~

Following is the unedited transcript of my niece, Lindsey Giancola's experience reproduced with her permission. Names have been changed by request.

On June 30, 2008, Jean Farrel and I left Pinellas county to vacation with her family on the opposite coast of Florida - in Cocoa Beach. Jean came to pick me up at ten o'clock. Since we were going on a big trip, we stopped to get her oil changed. They came out and told Jean she had a bubble in her tire and that means that it could pop at any moment but she and I wanted to get on the road so we told them that we would get it fixed later. We called her mom to tell her what was going on and asked her to pray for us and her mom told us to get the tire fixed. We argued it with her but eventually went to get it fixed. The tire was completely replaced and we were on the road by eleven thirty. Jean and I were on 14 and we heard a loud noise. Jean asked what it was and I said I think the tire popped.

The traffic situation was unfortunate. We were halfway past a semi truck on the right and there was a car on the front left and back left of our car. We were in the middle left of the four lanes of traffic.

Jean swerved right then swerved back left causing the car to spin into the left lane. I immediately thought in my mind "can Jean handle this?" and began shouting in heavenly tongues as we spun through traffic. At one point we were facing 14 traffic head on. We spun one more time making it two spins. The back left of the car hit the guardrail and then the front left hit also. Jean hit the brakes with the right front tire (Where I was sitting) right before the roadside and all we could see was a cloud of orange smoke around us. I immediately grabbed my head and touched all over feeling for blood. Jean then turned to me and I asked her if she was bleeding and if she was all right she nodded her head yes I asked her if I was bleeding she shook her head no. Two cars pulled over as Jean and I got out of the car. My door would not open so I crawled over the console and through the driver's side. I was weak so I squatted down prayed to God and thanked him and then waited to see if I was going to throw up. I then stood up and leaned against the guardrail as Jean began to talk to the gentlemen that stopped to help us. One had told us he called 911 immediately because he saw how bad the accident was, thinking we should be in critical condition. The ambulance came, asked if we were okay, and stayed for about five minutes to make sure we were going to be all right. We then proceeded with the process of calling our

Planting Seeds: The Art of Witnessing • 69

parents, answering questions, and figuring out what we should do. Sure enough, we saw that the brand new tire had popped. We then began to go through the emotions of confusion, anger, and disbelief. However, never once did we cry or get upset. We both stayed extremely calm as if nothing had happened. The officer took us to a nearby Starbucks while we waited for Jean's parents to drive two hours to pick us up. While we were in there we discussed everything. I said I feel weird that we are okay because while we were spinning I was prepared to spend it in a hospital. I told her how I told my dad how amazed I was at how she handled the car. We discussed that one of the men that pulled over to help us said he was amazed at how Jean handled the car. We talked how the officer was surprised at Jean's driving ability also telling us that the car should have flipped. We soon began to laugh at the situation and I said "Did you hear me shouting in tongues?" And she said "No, I could only hear you telling me what to do." I told her "No Jean I never once told you what to do; I clearly remember everything. I am positive I was shouting in tongues. It is an impulse I get in bad situations." She said "Lindsey, you said Left! Right! Let go of the wheel! BRAKE!" We both looked at each other and she said "I must have heard the directions of what to do through your tongues."

Fast forward to the Ford Dealership. The employee doing the estimate on Jean's car said, "I don't know how you did it but this car should have flipped. You must have some NASCAR in your blood." If we are keeping score that is 3 men telling a 18 year old girl they are impressed with her driving.

Jean and I both are completely fine now. We took ibuprofen before we went to bed that night, and again in the morning and neither of us have needed it since. Jean does not remember the crash as vividly as I do so her shock factor is fine but if I try to think about it too hard I get shaken up again. All I have to say is this was a miracle. There is absolutely no argument about it. I was there. I remember it all perfectly. I will not allow anyone to tell me otherwise or try to distort this miracle. I cannot keep people from doubting this but I know God was in complete control of everything. I have thanked God for my life every day. He truly has awakened me to his power and his glory.

This is my story. This is my testimony. He is my God.

CHAPTER 9

NEVER GIVE UP

---

[13]And now these three remain: faith, hope and love. But the greatest of these is love. 1 Cor. 13:13 (NIV)

1 Corinthians 13 is considered by most Christians as the LOVE scripture and for good reason. It describes what love is. It tells us that love is patient and kind. It does not envy or boast. It is not proud nor dishonors others. It is not self-seeking and is slow to anger. It keeps no records of wrong doing. Love does not like evil but likes truth. Love protects, trusts, hopes, and perseveres.

I also call it the NEVER GIVE UP scripture. It holds such promise for ours and future generations. FAITH, HOPE and LOVE, believe it or not, cannot be separated. In other words, you can't have one without the others. To a Christian we count on our faith to bring us hope. We look to hope to help us and other Christians get better. We pray because we love and hope our prayers will be answered. We understand the answer could be no.

Another way to look at it is, if you have no faith, why pray? If you have no hope, why pray? And if you have no love there is definitely no reason to pray. This is what witnessing is all about, giving HOPE. Spreading the good word about the love of Jesus and all the love He has and continues to give can only be done with 1 Corinthians 13 as one of our guides.

When witnessing you may find there seems to be no hope for someone. You try and try again to get through to them, but it seems useless. I feel certain that as a Christian, you may stop trying to witness to that person for a while but you don't stop praying. If you stop praying, you have given up.

Allow me to share with you how I dealt with this concept when I was a therapist. If a client and I had been working on an area of concern for the client, and the client had not been making any progress, I guess I could have scolded them for not trying. The client and I had spent a number of sessions trying to work on some methods of dealing with the problem the client was having. Every time the client returned for the next session, they had a lot of excuses as to why they had not put into practice what we had talked about the previous session. Like I said earlier, I could have scolded them for not trying but what good would that have done. I would just ask them, "Has the situation you're in improved?" Of course the answer would be No. At one point I would have to make a decision to discontinue the sessions with my client. I would discuss it with my supervisor and then say to my client something like the following: "Ms. Jones we have been working on a number of different ways to handle your concern. Why don't you take another look at some of the ideas we have been working on and when you think you are ready to put one into practice or if you come up with a new idea, give me a call to set up a another appointment."

Have I given up? No. I just let the client know that I still had a concern for her, but she just might need to take some time to see what her options were and what she could do about them. I would be only a phone call away. If they had not called back within a reasonable amount of time, I would contact them just to see how they were doing. At that time, they could make another appointment with me if they wanted to.

A medical doctor has a little different situation when dealing with a terminal patient. However, in most cases, the attending physician who has to inform the family of their love ones condition has tried every possible treatment to cure the patient. This includes getting others doctor's opinions and ideas on what might be done to save their patient. It is not unusual for the doctor to suggest that the family get a second opinion if they wish. The doctor is not giving up. If it is determined that the patient is going to die, most doctors will recommend the patient be placed in a hospice program. Believe it or not, this is not necessarily a give up suggestion. Sure there will be no more curing treatment offered the patient, but the hospice programs by design offer quality of life up until the patient dies. During that time anything can happen to include miracles.

Sometimes, as Christians, we need to plant the seeds and then let the Lord take over. That does not mean we walk away from the people we are witnessing to. It just means we are not going to force the situation. As the example above suggests, I can't force my client to get better. Neither can we force the people we are witnessing to, to become Christians.

It is so sad to think that a little child in a hospital may die because the parents do not believe and want no part of believing. But we Christians never give up. We can still pray for that child. When I pray, I always ask God to protect and save, if you will, some child or children that are being neglected or abused. I do not know them but I figure they need someone to pray for them, so why not me. I feel confident that the Lord honors my prayers. I also pray for that person or persons who need a prayer to get the through a tough situation. I ask the Lord if it be His will that they know that it was divine intervention that got them through it.

I always wonder who the non-believers turn to in time of trouble. Do they just HOPE all will go well? If they have a sick child, do they just HOPE they will be all right? If they are going on a trip, do they just HOPE they will arrive alive? You can use this HOPE to witness.

Ask the person who is hoping the child will be all right if he or she would like to you pray for the child. If they say no, tell them that it certainly won't hurt the situation they are facing and it might even help. If they say no but thank you, pray anyway. THAT'S WHAT WE DO.

It hurts our heart to realize that someone may not experience eternal life with Jesus and the joy we feel as Christians. But because of 1 Corinthians 13 which is found in the BIBLE, the inspired word of God, we NEVER GIVE UP. How wonderful this verse that speaks of FAITH, HOPE and LOVE. I do not see how anyone can argue against such beautiful words. They will try and lose.

Once again I remind you what Paul said in Galatians 6:9; "Let us not become weary in doing good, for at the proper time we will reap a harvest if we do not give up." (NIV) So let us not GIVE UP.

CHAPTER 10

IWWJ

[15]Blessed are those who have learned to acclaim you,
who walk in the light of your presence, Lord.
Psalm 89:15

The Lord put on my heart to add this chapter. He has
been wonderful about helping with this book. But He
has also made me aware that to be a good witness, I must
also walk continually with Him.

You are aware that the initials "WWJD" means What
Would Jesus Do? This is a great question to ask yourself
before making a decision or acting on a situation that
is set before you. I have another set of initials I would
like you to consider, "IWWJ". It is a statement that you
should make to yourself every minute of the day and
proclaim it when you witness. What does it stand for?
I'm Walking With Jesus.

What does it mean to walk with someone? First
when you walk with family member or friend, you are

with them. You are in their presence and you are not alone. Second, you are going in the same direction. Ever notice when you depart from the walk even slightly you start drifting apart. If you turn around and walk in the opposite direction, you are really separating yourself from them. And third, most of the time you are sharing with that individual you are walking with. You are talking about things you enjoy talking about. You are getting to know each other better.

Friendship is a wonderful thing. Being in the presence of a friend allows you to feel better. You also have the feeling of security. It is very rare you will walk with someone you do not like. If you have to walk with someone like that, very little is said, but at the same time it could be a great opportunity to witness.

Think about your walk with Jesus. He is your friend. You will have a lot to talk about. You certainly want to be going where He is going and you are in His presence. You feel secure. Jesus does not want anyone or anything to hurt you. At times the path gets very rough and you think all is lost, that is when He carries you. There was a poem called "Footprints" (author unknown). Find it somewhere and you will see what I mean. The point is, He is always there to comfort you in times of trouble and heartache.

As I have said before, you are not alone when you are walking with someone. In today's world, the word loneliness has a lot of different meanings - not fitting in, being bullied, being neglected, being forgotten, and just plain being alone - just to name a few of the meanings. Loneliness crosses all generations. Loneliness is not just an old age problem, it can effect everyone.

I noticed that everyone that called me on the suicide hot line was alone. Thank God, literally, for them calling the hot line. I never lost a person who called the hot line. Neither did the other therapists. Now before you start thinking we were the best therapists in the world, let me point out to you, the person calling really did not want to die. Believe me, if they wanted to die they would not have bothered. They would have just killed themselves.

In Chapter 6 "Witnessing in Difficult Situations," I mentioned that it was important that you remain with the person you believe might want to kill themselves or get them to a place where they can get additional help, but do not leave them alone. One of the biggest problems we had with dealing with suicidal people on the hot line was getting them help. We could not put them on hold while we tried to get them help. I would stay on the phone, sometimes for hours, waiting for someone to come into the house so I could talk with them and let them know how to help the person that I had been talking with. During normal office hours, I could get my secretary to call a family member or even the police to get someone out to the person's house to help them. I have even sent someone from the office to help.

Being alone is very real. It is important to let the

person you are witnessing to know that they are not alone. You are with them and certainly Jesus is with them. Once they begin their walk with Him, they are in His presence and they are not alone.

From time to time you may find yourself (I know I do) acting in a way that might not be considered "Christ like." That might be a good time to ask yourself, "Am I walking with Jesus?" A question we must continue to ask ourselves when we also ask "WWJD?"

The point I am trying to make is that this book was written to give you some ideas that might assist you in witnessing to others. We also must remind ourselves that we must always walk with the Lord. If we cannot walk with Him we certainly cannot walk with others and witness to them.

IWWJ is a great way to start a witness conversation. At this point I feel the need to tell you what the Lord has put on my heart as the result of writing this chapter (another Wow You're Good moment). I felt the call to get bracelets made that have IWWJ on the top half of the bracelet and Psalm 89:15 on the bottom half. I ordered 500 of them (to begin with) and then He told me to "get them out there" (the bracelets). I told Him that I felt I needed confirmation. So, like Gideon and the fleece (see Judges 6:36-40), I sort of challenged Him to give me an obvious sign. I was at the aviation museum, where I volunteer as a tour guide, wearing my IWWJ bracelet. A gentleman came up to the tour guide desk and noticed my bracelet. I told him what the IWWJ meant and gave him a bracelet and card and gave him one for his wife. He read the card which explains what the bracelet is all about and then he said "You need to get them out there." During our conversation I found out he was a retired chaplain. I ordered some more bracelets and had additional cards printed up. This time with a message on the cards for youths. I then asked the Lord, "now how am I going to get them out there?" (Now it gets even better.)

The next Thursday morning, after I had asked the question, was our Methodist men's breakfast. We meet every Thursday. One of our members showed up with a young man from the Fellowship of Christian Athletes organization. The member said "George, I know I have the devotional this morning so I brought along a young man to tell us about a special event he is going to put on here in Enterprise for the athletes in our area." I informed him he did not have the devotional this morning, I did. However, I was more than happy to let this gentleman talk. I listened to what he had to say and then waited for the opportunity to give him a bracelet and card. I then asked him if I could pass them out at the rally. He said I could. The night of the rally my wife, grandson, and I passed out 496 bracelets and cards to both adults and youths. What a blessing. I have no idea how many more I have passed out since then. One additional thing I have done is to make a book mark for children to go along with their bracelet. The following is what is printed on the adult's cards, the youth cards, and the children's bookmarks. Everyone who receives a bracelet also receives a card or bookmark to go with it.

The Adult card says IWWJ (I'm Walking With Jesus). This is your witness bracelet. When someone asks, "What does IWWJ mean?" and they will, take the opportunity to tell them about your walk with Jesus. Also let this bracelet remind you to be true to your walk with Him. When you walk with someone you are in their presence. You are their friend and you are having a conversation with them. What a wonderful relationship you are having with Jesus when you walk with Him. Psalm 89:15 says "Blessed are those who have learned to acclaim you, who walk in the light of your presence, Lord."

The Youth card says IWWJ (I'm Walking With Jesus). This is your witness bracelet. When someone asks you what does IWWJ mean, and they will, take the opportunity to tell them about your walk with Jesus. Also let this bracelet remind you to be true to your walk with Him. If one of your friends asks you to take drugs, get drunk, or engage in other non-Christian activities, point to your bracelet and say; "I'm walking with Jesus and I am already committed." When you walk with someone you are in their presence and are usually having a conversation with them. Psalm 89:15 says "Blessed are those who have learned to acclaim you, who walk in the light of your presence, Lord."

The Children's bookmark says IWWJ (I'm Walking With Jesus). This is your witness bracelet. When someone asks what it means, you tell them. When you walk with Jesus you are with Him. Your are going the same way He is. If you feel bullied or pushed around, just point to your bracelet and say "I'm walking with Jesus and He loves me just the way I am." If someone wants you to do something that Jesus would not like you to do, again point to your bracelet and say "I'm walking with Jesus and He does not want me to do that." Remember, Jesus is someone you will always want to be with and He will always want to be with you. Psalm 89:15 says, "Blessed are those who have learned to acclaim you, who walk in the light of your presence, O Lord."

One additional note about IWWJ. I gave some bracelets to some children and I asked them what they thought IWWJ meant. One answered "I Will Worship Jesus." Not bad. What a wonderful additional meaning for IWWJ. We also need to keep that meaning in mind when someone wants you to stray from your beliefs. God is great, is He not?

------------ CHAPTER 11 ------------

HARVEST

[9]Let us not become weary in doing good, for at the proper time we will reap a harvest if we do not give up. [10]Therefore, as we have opportunity, let us do good to all people, especially to those who belong to the family of believers. Gal. 6:9-10 (NIV)

It is hoped that as the result of reading this book you will have a better understanding of how to witness. Group interaction is advised, and discussing witnessing techniques can be a great help. The key point I wanted to present is that you witness like Jesus did, and that is with love and patience. Try to understand the person's situation you are witnessing to so that you can be effective in your witnessing. Jesus went to the people where they were. His teachings were about the times and situations people found themselves in. He also witnessed by example. His examples alone lead many to follow Him. His dying on the cross for our sins was the ultimate example. Without His sacrifice, we would not join Him in heaven.

We plant seeds so others will have that experience at the end of their life journey. How successful we are we may never know. But the thought of helping someone find a wonderful life not only here on earth but for all eternity is truly wonderful.

At some point the Lord may show you the fruits of your labor. When that time comes, He will say "Well done good and faithful servant." Will you stop there? I would hope not. The Bible says in Mat. 9:37-38, [37]Then he said to his disciples, "The harvest is plentiful but the workers are few. [38]Ask the Lord of the harvest, therefore, to send out workers into his harvest field." (NIV) There is a lot of work still to be done.

I cannot express how blessed I have felt writing this book. I have prayed about it and asked the Lord to guide me. I truly believe He has done so. When you talk about witnessing, the most important thing to remember is to pray and ask the Lord to be your guide. I end this writing like I started, with scripture. God bless you.

[7] It is not for you to know the times or dates the Father has set by his own authority. [8] But you will receive power when the Holy Spirit comes on you; and you will be my witnesses in Jerusalem, and in all Judea and Samaria, and to the ends of the earth. Acts 1:7-8 (NIV)

ENRICHING THE SOIL

Chapter 1
SOMETHING TO THINK ABOUT

1. Think of more "You just don't get it ..." and "You will surely miss something ..." and discuss them.
2. What are your thoughts about the "Whatever man fears or does not understand ..." statement?
3. Discuss the "Human dilemma statement."

Chapter 2
AN OVERVIEW OF WITNESSING

1. Are you required to witness as a Christian?
2. When you witness, how confident are you?
3. Why do you think Christians find it difficult to witness?

Chapter 3
PLANTING SEEDS

1. Did Jesus have an easy time planting seeds? Explain.
2. List some of the different methods Jesus used to plant seeds.
3. What can you do to plant seeds?

Chapter 4
NOT AGAINST FLESH AND BLOOD

1. What are some other organizations or groups not mentioned here that might need to be witnessed to?
2. If someone comes to your door that has a belief not grounded in the Bible and wants to give you one of their tracks, how might you handle the situation?
3. To what degree, if any, do we have the right to judge these individuals or their belief systems?

Chapter 5
PREPARING THE SOIL

1. If you had to list some key words or attributes that would help you become a better witness, what would they be?
2. What does listening provide you?
3. Why should you have a full grasp of the Bible?

Chapter 6
THE ART OF WITNESSING

1. How can personal experiences help you when witnessing?
2. Do you feel getting angry at times can help in witnessing? Why?
3. What is the difference between having a passion about something and anger?

Chapter 7
HOW TO WITNESS IN DIFFICULT SITUATIONS

1. What would you say are some of the most important attributes a person needs when witnessing in difficult situations?
2. What part do emotions play when witnessing in difficult situations?
3. Have you found yourself witnessing in a difficult situation? Would you be willing to share that experience?

Chapter 8
WOW! YOU'RE GOOD

1. What miracles have you witnessed in your lifetime?
2. Why do you think it is so difficult for people to believe in miracles?
3. How has the Lord spoken to you?

Chapter 9
NEVER GIVE UP

1. Are there situations that may require the discontinuing of witnessing? Explain.
2. How would you deal with a person who just won't listen?
3. How far is too far when it comes to witnessing?

Chapter 10
HARVEST

1. Why do you think witnessing is more difficult today than in the past?
2. How does it feel to know someone has accepted Jesus Christ as their Lord and Savior?
3. How important is it that you know your witnessing was successful?

REFERENCES

Broocks, R. (2013). *God's Not Dead.* Nashville, TN: W Publishing Group an Imprint of Thomas Nelson.

Broocks, R., Habermas, G. R., & Broocks, R. (2016). *Man, myth, messiah: answering history's greatest question.* Nashville, TN: W Publishing Group, an imprint of Thomas Nelson.

Enterprise State Secular Student Alliance (ESSSA) [ESSSA Information Flyer]. (n.d.). Enterprise State Community College, Enterprise, AL.

Kendrick, A., & Kendrick, S. (Directors). (2015). *War Room* [Motion picture]. Tri Star Pictures.

Stand up for your rights. (n.d.). Retrieved February 06, 2017, from http://www.atheists.org/aboutus/history

The Bible: New International Version. (1984). Colorado Springs, CO: International Bible Society.

Thrasher, T. (2016). *God's Not Dead 2*. Tyndale.

Wallace, J. W. (2013). *Cold-case Christianity: a homicide detective investigates the claims of the Gospels.* Colorado Springs, CO: David C Cook.

NOTES